The Boy Who Nearly Won the Texaco Art Competition

The Boy Who Nearly Won
the Texaco Art Competition

JOE KANE

**NEW
ISLAND**

THE BOY WHO NEARLY WON THE TEXACO ART COMPETITION
first published 2007
by New Island
2 Brookside
Dundrum Road
Dublin 14
www.newisland.ie

Copyright © Joe Kane 2007

The author has asserted his moral rights.

ISBN 978-1-905494-57-6

British Library Cataloguing Data. A CIP catalogue record for this
book is available from the British Library.

Book design by Inka Hagen
Printed in the UK by Athenaeum Press Ltd., Gateshead, Tyne & Wear

New Island received financial assistance from
The Arts Council (An Chomhairle Ealaíon), Dublin, Ireland.

10 9 8 7 6 5 4 3 2 1

Acknowledgements

Grateful acknowledgement is made to the following.

Journals:
The Shop, The New Writer, Envoi, Black Mountain Review, Fire, The Times, The New York Review of Books and *Fortnight.*

Anthologies:
The Open Door Book of Poetry, The Arvon Anthology 04, The Literary Experience 06, Sunday Miscellany 06 and *Lifelines 06.*

RTÉ has broadcast several poems from this collection.

'The Boy Who Nearly Won the Texaco Art Competition' won the Duncan Lawrie first prize in the Arvon International Poetry Competition. 'Half Labrador' was awarded second prize in the Smurfit Samhain International Poetry Competition 2004. The collection was awarded third prize in the Patrick Kavanagh Awards 2004, a group of poems was nominated for the American Pushcart Prize XXX 2005 and was short-listed for the Listowel Poetry Collection prize.

Thanks to the Poets' House, Maggie Dan's and the Bedlam Writers' Group.

Special thanks also to Phyl Ó Donnell, Cathal Ó Searcaigh and Ted Deppe.

for Anne and Joanne

'Moontalk', for Ted and Annie Deppe
'Wood-Sorrel Kiss', for Anne
'Traffic Jams', for Paul and Bella Stewart
'Half Labrador', for Mark Meaney
'Dodder', for Joanie Stewart and Mary Hanna
'The Boy Who Nearly Won the Texaco Art Competition', for Ted Hughes
'Benediction', for Bob and Kate
'St. John's Ward', for Chris and Rita
'Empties', for Phyl Ó Donnell
'Song of My Amazing Trousers (and a red shirt)', for Eamonn and Eithne Mc Carthy
'Mesmerise', for Joanne
'Torture by Terzanelle', for Nigel McLoughlin
'The Waves of Tory', for Cathal Ó Searcaigh

Contents

The Boy Who Nearly Won the Texaco Art Competition

he took a large sheet
of white paper and on this
he made the world an african world
of flat topped trees and dried grasses
and he painted an elephant in the middle
and a lion with a big mane and several giraffes
stood over the elephant and some small animals to fill
in the gaps he worked all day had a bath this was saturday

on sunday he put six jackals
in the world and a great big snake
and buzzards in the sky and tickbirds
on the elephants back he drew down blue
from the sky to make a river and got the elephants
legs all wet and smudged and one of the jackals got drowned
he put red flowers in the front of the picture and daffodils in the bottom corners
and his dog major chewing a bone and mrs murphys two cats tom and jerry
and milo the milkman with a cigarette in the corner of his mouth
and his merville dairy float pulled by his wonder horse trigger
that would walk when he said click click and the holy family
in the top right corner with the donkey and cow
and sheep and baby jesus and got the 40A bus
on monday morning in to abbey street to hand
it in and the man on the door said
thats a sure winner

1

Discover Donegal

The brochure says:
            don't
        dream,
                go…

There's a generic cliff-face
and the face of a woman that might be generic.
The sky is blue, the sea a darker blue
but not ominous. A red flag marks
where you should aim the golf ball.

The face is tilted to the cliff
with breasts mountainous but slightly concealed.
She might be pondering on the beauty
of *here*; her skin is taut from her uplifted chin.
She is naked except for the word:
                dream
one eye half closed, a near-away look
that says:
        I must be visited…

She has enhanced nipples—this is purely speculative
as I'm not a golfer—you could
hang your duffle-coat on one, if this were winter.

But the winter it is past
        and this is:
                Your Free Guide to…
                The Towns
                Villages
                Attractions
                & Amenities
                of Donegal

A Box of Books

Colm Tóibín's *The Master* came by post
with six who-dunnits, three poetry books,
the *Listowel Writers' Week, Winners,*
The Beau, an annual publication of literature and art
(now defunct), four proof copies, and a cookery book.
Out of this eclectic gathering, my dog selected to eat
The Master. I've met Colm Tóibín, and I don't think
he would be overly upset, he might,
of course, do one of those Cork things...
It's not Tóibín I'm concerned about, it's the other fella,
James. He's been long dead, never met him,
but I've met someone who claimed kinship.
I wasn't being inquisitive. She said:
'I'm a descendant of the James Brothers.'
I naïvely asked: 'Jesse and Frank?'
Well, her nose went in the air as if someone
somewhere had cancelled gravity
(I wondered could it be congenital)
and this from a woman who had just been
skinny dipping off Tory Island
and had just enthralled one of my friends
in the confines of a four-berth, drop-keel,
gaff-rigged, trailer-sailor: before breakfast.
So I thought, Henry's the one likely to be a bit pissed;
I set about repairing the book.
The first ten pages got the worst of it.

Example: page eight, upper right:

> *His wife was agreeable while the p...*
hearted while he was suspicious, and...
while he pouted in the corner.

Grand words but how to fill in the gaps.
Dilemma: do I follow James, or Tóibín.

Or there again—
Should I be mucking about with a book
that's likely to win the Man Booker Prize?
Should I have remonstrated with the dog?
Should I have looked through the morning-
mist at James's aisling naked at Tory?
Should I keep a dog that can't tell the difference
between a who-dunnit and a work of art?

Traffic Jams

The women of Falcarragh
dance naked at the crossroads on Fridays
making garlands of tangerines and seedless grapes,
hanging them around the necks of strange men, from the place
of the leaping dogs, Sixmile Town, the Cobh of Cork.

(I knew a man from Bavaria, who gave up his
Vorsprung durch Technik for Fridays in Falcarragh.)
Unloading men from the cabs of their trucks and bread vans,
making a pillar of their clothes. Anointing white bodies
with extra virgin olive oil, massaging it in from head to toe:

The women of Falcarragh dance from the knees up.
Falcarragh men stand hushed in doorways, mutter
imprecations to a God of small miracles.

These women know their Gods as well
as their fresh fruit. Lugh of the long hand,
Balor of the eye of truth, powerful irredentist gods,
who slumber in the sound beyond the isle
of the fair cow, waiting for show time.

When they have brought Falcarragh to a standstill,
gather up aubergines, kerr pinks and mangetouts,
salute the lone Garda who has been hiding beyond
An Glas Gaibhlean, they feck off home.

Half Labrador

A dog mooches into the yard all head and ribcage;
You shoo him out twice but he's back again,

And because you never grew into the hero
You dreamt you would, you throw him some scraps.

He knows he has found a stray heart and within
A week he's lying by the range, ordering in takeaways—

Looking like a bull calf in clover, yawning when Attenborough
Comes on the television, wrestling you for the remote control,

Relenting as *Coronation Street*'s signature tune fills the kitchen.
You wonder was the malnutrition a trick

But are too busy trying to stop him taking liberties with the cat
And retrieving splinters of furniture from the vacuum cleaner.

He has such a soft mouth:
Monday and Thursday he takes the delivered

Carton of milk from the back door to the front
And you begin to think, *good boy,* but don't say it aloud.

One Wednesday you find a carton at the front door
and wonder which neighbour is drinking black coffee?

A week before Christmas, a present of a hen—not a feather
Out of place, you later tell—it's one of Neilie Doherty's,

So you sit in his kitchen trying to press the price of a good layer
On Neilie, as the two of you drink strong tea and he tells you about

All the dogs he's had, mostly good, some duds. And then there's
Mrs McCallion's goose that had the good sense to play dead.

And after three years he's half trained and the postman
Has taken to stepping out of his van, tapping him on the head—

Man dear, but that's a wild civil dog. So that's the way it is.
He's either stretched in front of the range or in full flight

After giant red deer…and one day you're distracted talking
To a friend, and he flies past you out under a bus

And he's burst down the middle, his beating heart
Jumps out on the tarmac towards you—

Beating, beating, beating, and, those who witness this, stand memerised.
Your neighbor Jim out checking his sheep, Mickey Sharkey

Who has stopped by for a chat, a woman whose name
You don't know, the bus driver; all stare at this desperation.

Gathering up the still beating heart
You put it in the wheelie bin out of the cats' way;

Go looking for the wheelbarrow and eventually
Find it; push it back up the lane where Mickey is sluicing

Down the road with buckets of water; and the two of you land Oscúr
In the barrow. The busman is still there, and he says:

I've a grand litter of pups, I'll bring you down the pick o' them
As soon as I'm finished work.
Ahh, no thanks…

I push the barrow into the lower field, the one with the rushes,
Dig a big hole, tip him in, and backfill. A clump of monbretia on top.

The Waves of Tory

I am the beached stones of the Backstrand
you have made me what I am:
you have rolled and pounded,
tossed and tested, polished and pierced me.

I am the grained sand of the Backstrand
you have made me what I am:
you have ground and granulated,
sieved and settled, tuned and fine-tuned me.

I am the dead seagull of the Backstrand
you have made me what I am:
you have fed and fleshed,
preened and plucked, raked and racked me.

I am gannet memory
I am seal through the water
I am bladderwrack drying
I am sea-urchin lonely
I am caressed
I am washed
I am invaded
I am absolved
I am blessed
I am obliterated
by The Waves of Tory.

Moontalk

This constant quiet
at the edge, room to speak:
say dune, say deep,
say sand, say water,
a finite future,
the cleansing sweep,
clutch marram-grass anchor,
speak whitehorse,
speak water, speak night-air.

Travel between grains,
feel the comfort of beach,
roll with the contours
of spring and neap.
Stake a claim
on the tide-line:
on strength of sprat,
on dive of gannet,
on seal memory.
Caress this ever-
changing conversation.

Stepping Out

Leave this land forever:
carry no clay
between your toes
step on to the great whale-road
and travel under the shadow of gannet
to where the sun suckles the sea.
You will not need wings or faith in transubstantiation
to achieve balance and buoyancy
through the everlasting music
the thrum thrum of the ocean bed.
Pink rays will be the poles of your magnetic field
and somewhere between water and no-water
somewhere between tomorrow's grains of hope
you'll find a niche in the eye of a gilled rainbow:
rain will still be rain
salt will be salt and sand forever pretending.

Alternate Lives

Took your time, there was no rush,
young sapling in the photograph, 1887.
Bending and swaying with the northwesterly.
Today, stiff and broken-limbed,
rot set in your heart. Now,
the last to wake up in spring,
first to sleep in autumn. Your doom
held in the trough of some future storm,
bringing you to ground to complete the cycle.
Good only for the kitchen range.

But you could've been a contender:
taken down in your prime
waxed and left to dry slowly
trimmed and dressed,
ready for the workshop:
the right hands would have found
the fruit within, dense, flexible, responsive,
spoke-shaved to its final shape,
sanded for the hand of a virtuoso.
The first puck of the *sliotar* would have told all.

Metaphor

Your naked lover asks you to open the window
to let the stale air out, and just as the sash weight drops
a pipistrelle flies in to add a few more moments of frenzy.

You would rather get back to bed
but she says she won't sleep
with that thing banging about the room,

and though half an hour ago you were reciting
love poems to her, this really pisses you off, so you
stand like an eejit with shirt stretched between arms,

now bouncing on the bed to try and deflect it,
hoping its radar is working: a vague recollection
from boy scouts, or was it David Attenborough…

She was clawing the back off you a few moments ago,
now she's groaning at your antics, and at the sight
of your disappearing manhood, and for no reason
that you can fathom the bat escapes out the window.

Not Me

I have fifty cup-hooks, brass-effect,
and can't figure out what to do with them.
They fit into a small plastic bag
no bigger than a closed fist.
I've thought of throwing them in the bin
but it seems such a wilful act, maybe
better to leave them on the worktable;
but I also know that I will keep coming
across them, and each time I'll have a decision
to make. And the thought of fifty cup-hooks,
taking up time that I could be devoting
to state-of-the-world questions,
or even what to do with five
partly empty paint cans
that sit under my worktable?
So you see the pickle I'm in. I could
ask your opinion, but then again you would
tell a friend, and he/she would of course make
a better story of it down the pub, and before
you know it I'm the fall guy in a story that
grows and grows into a little bit of our
history, then into a myth,
maybe into a children's bedtime tale:
like Jack and the Beanstalk
or the Three Little Pigs, or any of the other
delinquent characters that haunt my
wakin' hours, so I ask my self, do I want
to sacrifice my version of reality
to be a bit part in a parable?

False-Face

When a man has lost his smile,
his sense of humour, not to mention
the loose change in his pocket:
it's just as well he has his false-face.
Johnny has learned to master
his madness with measure.
He measures out time in units of seven.

Rising at seven, working till seven,
on the seventh day he goes mad
in an I-don't-care-if-I-never-wake-up-
from-this-madness kinda mad.
For six days he has pulled on his false-face
on rising, today he leaves it at home,
or leaves it in place until the juice kicks in.

Johnny lives in silence,
except when he speaks in tongues.
A barely audible whispered fuuuck…
a prayer rising from his gut,
a draught turning to storm
louder and louder,
angrier and angrier.

Cuuunt…
And when he's in full flow
he's asked to leave the pub,
and he wants to fight the barman
but the barman knows
this is Johnny's mad day:
and we all need our day of rest.

Drinking Beer in Bed

Three storeys above the backyard
and the doorbell rings.

Pull up my trousers
as soon as I hear a car in the lane

so as to look casual when I open the door.
Show me the way to Amarillo,

I hope I'm asked, but again
it's 'Do you know Sharkey's Joinery?'

or 'Can you tell me where the leprechaun
maker is to be found?' Never a mention of

Anne Marie who waits for me. Down
three flights I fall, to give lost people directions.

Saviour of wrong turns,
show me road signs that little boys can't

swing round to send me back to here:
Show me the way to Amarillo.

Her Husband As an Incandescent Light?

The North winds blow thunderbolts—
negative electrons gather in grass
to fasten on falling stars.

Gods stand at Valhalla's gates
arguing the toss, shooting the breeze.
Each flash, each Voltaire of illumination,

seeks its way to the centre of this moment:
re-emerges writing messages in glyphs
too bright to fathom.

He wears Christmas tree lights for bright relief
in January, he likes the chance to glow.
Switching to flashing mode to dazzle,
more often he's happy in the flow.

February's modulations bestow
a sense of rhythm. When footfalls
quake and batteries are low, he grabs
the jump-leads and plugs into an alternating

current: positive to the right, negative
to the left. His feet will earth him.
Throw the switch and, before darkness
takes back the night, he's brilliant.

Nobody Remarked on the Unseasonable Weather

And there were thunderstorms of knives
slashing down out of the sky
and so many broad backs
to receive them.

Moya the bank manager
took hers in the left shoulder
and sat at the word processor
dripping blood over overdue accounts.

The ninety-two-year-old ex-schoolteacher
got it in the right leg, just above the knee,
she had gone across the road
to pick up the *Irish Times* and a carton of milk.

Nobody remarked on the unseasonable weather.

Two lovers holding hands in the porch of the Shamrock Lodge
were amazed to see that both of them were pierced
in the left breast with identical boning knives,
moulded black handle, by F.N. Nix. Dublin.

And from an tSean-Bhearaic
to Seamus Danny's
there wasn't a man, woman or child
not fatally wounded

and nobody remarked on the unseasonable weather.

18

Torture by Terzanelle

We are sitting in Gort a' Choirce tryin'
to scan the workings of a terzanelle.
This is torture by Nigel Mc Loughlin.

Cramped bums on hard forms, is this not hell,
our brain cells scream for an anesthetic
to scan the workings of a terzanelle.

Lured here with talk of form, a shyster's trick:
no mention of Cheltenham or Aintree,
our brain cells scream for an anesthetic,

our bodies twitch: how long more will he be
extolling the worth of Lewis Turco.
No mention of Cheltenham or Aintree,

accumulators and almanacs. So,
to work out the value of complex form,
extolling the worth of Lewis Turco

(this end rhyming will never be the norm),
we are sitting in Gort a' Choirce tryin'
to work out the value of complex form:
This is torture by Nigel Mc Loughlin.

Mesmerise

The shock absorbers were shot.
We were heading for the Fiat dealership
One hundred miles away.
It was a sellers' market.

Ten new Puntos in the yard
Delivered the previous day.
Take your pick the salesman said,
And off he went.

What do you think
My daughter said
I like the green one
And the pink one
I like pink she said
So pink it was
We'll have the pink we said
We don't have pink
It's in the yard we said
We have green and blue
Black and yellow
And I think one red
Walked back to the yard
With the stock list
Yes he said
Green blue
Black yellow
And one red
That's pink we said
Look at the book
Red it says
So we bought red

iii

We have two hands, a left and a right:
Where do we hear touch?
We have two eyes, a left and a right:
Where do we feel sight?
We have two ears, a left and a right:
Where do we touch sound?

iv

In Donegal we look at the sky and say red
In January, when everything from the bay up
Is pink. Add a dash of aquamarine shooting
Through black. The purple wash of mountains

Surrounds us, but it's always pink that comes
From the ground, that takes the sky.
The sun is in the ground in January
And wants to have its say.

I write the Winter sky in Donegal and bottle it.
So next time I'm west of Inis Bó Finne
I'll toss it out there with the minkes and hope
The great whale-road takes it, my daughter, to you.

Janus

As the tide is rising on a New Year,
we read the results of what has gone
before, take the egg timer, turn it round,
fake the calculations for survival.

We would like to give an exact
measurement of our place,
tabulate, calibrate
and end up with a bottom line.

But we are more than the sum
of our disappointments—
we feel for the rhythm of a new day
and make our adjustments.

Wood-Sorrel Kiss

Lost under
whin and elderflower,
wood-sorrel kiss,
shade of
morning glory:

and hope
in ditch
and sheugh
in drain
in turlough
in muck
and midden
in claggy clay
in clabber
in mold of birch
in spring rivulet:

turning in ever
smaller circles,
finding my centre
at your core.

At Sixty

Looking through the wrong end of a telescope
To see a pinpoint of light
That illuminates nothing

You cradle the telephone
Today all your connections
Are broken

September winds blow
Black sky—a murder of crows—
How auguries grow

A Warning from Peter Samson in His Book *Writing Poems*

Shards:

> about the over-use
> of the word shards; it seems they are scattered
> about poems in all sorts of disguises
> rarely meaning what they are.
> And wasn't I delighted to find shards
> of reason in Moya Cannon's convincing poem,
> *Shards,* and although Moya is very accurate
> in her use of the word—shards,
> why would it give you indigestion
> if she had shattered its meaning.

Shards:

> what are you talking about Peter?
> Isn't language meant to change,
> to be in a state of flux.
> It's not that I don't like your book
> (blame this attempt on it if you like).

Shards:

> clay transformed by fire
> to something breakable:
> porous fragments of earthenware
> I have held in my hands,
> wondered at the vessel
> they once had faith in.

Shards:

> just another word for broken.

The Tree

From his mother he inherited a hazel wand,
The power of divination, and a dream.

From his father he inherited a thirst, a gold watch,
And an angry-tree.

The hazel wand came without instructions
But he found water in every step.

Dreams are what he made of rivers, lakes
Canals, abandoned quarries.

Books whetted his thirst, gave him a story line,
A place to be, where he could choose his name.

The gold watch he wore on special occasions,
Wound it if he wanted the time of day.

The tree in the end flamed into leaf
Would not be buried as he'd meant.

In the AM

The song asks: *why do you build me up*
buttercup baby just to let me down?

Who's messin' round with my brainwaves
that's what I want to know?
Who turned on the radio? How do I turn it off?
Stuck on a wave length called—difficult to dislodge
this crap song FM— I want an aria from Lakmé,
I want Fauré requiem, but all I get is buttercups, buttercups:
she loves me, she loves me not. If I'm to be haunted in the AM by FM
please let Ella *try a little tenderness.*
O Billie, how do I exorcise the DJ with the terminal play-list.

and worst of all
you never call baby when you say you will.

Empties

Perhaps glass remembers flame and fire
oxygen and flux, fume and furnace.

Perhaps silica remembers pressure and shear
melt and flow, molten potential.

Silica sands shift grains of super-
cooled liquid to imitate clear
solidity. Bottle-banks yield low
interest for form with ambition
to sit centre table. Liquid-containers
freed of purpose assuming botanical
identity, would rather court crocosmia
than hold juice of cranberry,
would rather fondle foxglove.

Empty bottles find roles not intended:
amber whiskey for Flanders poppy,
olive oil minds winter jasmine
in Scandinavian minus degrees.
Southern Sun seeks Guinness
waisted longneck to hold bougainvillea
tenderly, milk bottles range the globe
on J1,11's looking for elongated
eucalyptus, to linger below the
homogenised line.

ii

You stood in line empty to the neck
with dark nights full of dull stars
that never rose above the pavement.
The Milky Way trapped in a leaden
pothole-pool of oiled water. Lamp-
lit sodium vapour stole the shadows,
leaving separateness your only cover.

You stood, harvested dreams
from prisms of the mind, bent colours
of thought through the light of spent
stars, reflected fractured beginnings
in the glory-hole of creation. Light
is time in a bottle, hardened by the
untouchable northern aurora—
light, shape, and things.

Glass remembers flame and fire.
Silica remembers potential.

On a Slow Train to Thomastowm

On a slow train to Thomastown packed
with Christmas home-bound travellers,
in the one remaining space in the last carriage
I sit down. Just as I'm about to open my book,
the woman sitting diagonally opposite me asks,
no states. *You're the president:*
The president of Ireland.

I hesitate a moment (quietness in the carriage)
her hand shoots out, *Pleased to meet you Mr DeValera.*
I shake her hand, I blush. 'Ah...I...ah...you're mistaken.'
She doesn't say anything, the smile slips from her face.
She keeps looking at me, she knows with certainty
that she's right—*imagine mistaking someone*
for Mr DeValera—she doesn't believe me.

'Excuse me ma'am, I'm not Alan Rickman.'
No Mr DeValera, you're not Alan Rickman.
I sit uneasily reading, not able to concentrate,
a slight headache. At Kildare I enquire of her,
'Would you like a cup of tea, the restaurant car is open.'
She looks at me, *I'm sure if you mention it to the steward*
he'll organise that, she winks.

Kildare, an hour to go, ahem! 'Mr Lemass
is doing a good job in Leinster House,' I say.
She puts aside the handbag she's been clutching.
We set to discussing the weather and affairs of state.

Vivaldi's Stir-Fry

Spring

Stopped in for a sandwich, the surroundings
Took over: a poet was walking a tightrope

Between two sonnets. He proved he was a poet
When he stepped down to wrestle a crocodile. I complained

To the manager. He said, 'Poets are beyond my ken.'
Wasn't that rather Zen for a duty manager? Paper to hand,

His hands full of crocodile, I'll have whatever poem
Is penned in this hotel. I'll nail it to the door by autumn.

Summer

Waiting for lunch I listened to a man from Monaghan
Who bred the first Charolais herd in these parts:

'Grand animals but they're a bugger to calve.'
Did he think I was another refugee from the wedding

Breakfast in the lounge? Wanted to buy me a drink,
Told me his daughter hadn't spoken to him in twenty years—

No idea why, as he lowered his twelfth pint of the day.
Thanked him, told him I was just breaking my journey.

Autumn

Still hadn't found that poem – words eaten by a crocodile
Likely to be more digestible than a whole poet.

But I'm here at Nabokov's '*delicate meeting place*'
And if my pockets are full of wrinkled words

I'll keep them, perhaps mulch them around
Some tender roots,

After all, in the spring I couldn't tell my
Petrarch from Noah's ark.

Winter

Stopped in for a sandwich, the surroundings
Almost overwhelmed me: it wasn't just the toss-up

Between the Stir-Fry and the Fajitas. If this bar was human,
You might want to commit it for electro-convulsive therapy.

But I say give yourself to the music: what's not to enjoy
In a Greco-Roman-Georgian-Classical-Contortions-

With-a-faux-rustic-salt-of-the-earthenware-cast-iron-kettles-
On-the-shelf-can't-see-the-dirt-on-the-carpet sort of place?

Confluence

of rivers Tolka
and Tullaghobegley
where mineral rich
alluvial muds
settled to form
a delta of words
each layered gradation
an evolution
of spoken fossils,
tried and tested sounds
trapped by pressure.

Time compresses words
to slate, too brittle
for jackhammers.
Only the fine-tipped
nib of imagination
will dig them out.

Homage to Theodore Roethke

i

On First Reading *Words for the Wind*

You wanted to be finest hickory,
hafted to tempered steel, forging
casehardened words of crisp utility.

Digging your way to the root
you came upon a watercourse,
sat to drink. Asked the question,
are words the source of all rivers?

At the place of the Salmon
your words pulsate through me,
my ink stuttering to flow.

Deciding to prospect for words, rolled
a nugget in my left hand
reciting, the faith of our fathers—
dreamtime without end.

World without end
World without middle
World without beginning

ii

Unfinished World

There were too many questions for the worm,
and he hadn't got eyes for any of them.
The sound of time was always the same,
tock, tock, and the green leaves fell—

and the hum of empty stars filled his ears
and the thunder came and came again
and nothing touched him
and the green leaves fell

and big stones
turned to small stones
and the sea talked out of boredom
and sometime after dinner—

God fell asleep
with a glass of cheap port in his hand.

Again

I am at the point of pain
looking for the magic word
you say, again!
I am a four-year-old looking
into a garden of fear
you say, gladioli!
I am a seven-year-old sitting
on my master's knee
you say, age of reason!
I am a twelve-year-old knitting
a shield of pubic hair
you say, again!
I am a sixteen-year-old carrying
words I cannot read
you say, shout!
I am an eighteen-year-old swimming
in a vat of vomit
you say, carnation!
I am a young father looking
at the sky that burns
you say, mouth of fire!
I am at fifty *that final thing*
a man learning to sing,
you say, abracadabra.

Dodder

Aunt Mary kept six hens
For company, a cock for colour,
Under the Dodder river—
A pear tree for a roost,
A conger eel for a guard dog:
Aunt Mary took no chances.
  Aunt Mary is gone—
  The Dodder is still.

Aunt Mary kept a man for fun,
Never took his socks too seriously,
Under the Dodder river—
A man for fun,
A swan for a pillow:
Aunt Mary took no chances.
  Aunt Mary is gone—
  The Dodder is still.

Aunt Mary said God was good,
But never got around to praying,
Under the Dodder river—
A bottle of whiskey to recite,
A poem to imbibe:
Aunt Mary took no chances.
  Aunt Mary is gone—
  The Dodder is still.

Aunt Mary ate onions whole,
Belched, created whirlpools
Under the Dodder river—
A tongue that never blocked the sun,
A hand that never spancelled the moon:
Aunt Mary took no chances.
  Aunt Mary is gone—
  The Dodder is still.

How High Was the Steeple?

The scaffolding reached up and up
wrapped round the steeple;
we all wanted to climb
hand over hand
foot over foot

we weren't that stupid.
But we were surprised
when Mickey dropped
that God didn't catch him:
and him an altar boy

and wearing short trousers in sixth class
and white ankle socks
and calling his ma *Mummy*.
(We beat him up for that twice.)
And running into the Tin church

every chance he got: not
Sunday mass, Saturday confession,
Friday stations and Holy Days,
but every chance he got, the holy Joe.
We double-dog dared him

and he went up and up.
How high was the steeple?
John O'Shea said he screamed
all the way down,
bounced twenty feet back in the air

before he burst on the concrete blocks.
Mr Mc Ginley said Mickey fainted
just as he touched the cross at the very
tip top and fell to a mountain
of soft sand and went straight to heaven.

Rio Grande, Rio Tolka

We took the Tolka in 62,
wielding sticks and slings
we drove the Cabra hordes
beyond the river.

Davy Crockett
whispers in my ear,
Remember the Alamo.

Years later at San Antonio I read the letter
of a young man who rode seven weeks
across seven states
to pour his blood into our myth basket.

And the Daughters of the American Revolution
whisper in my ear,
Remember the Alamo.

Dreaming by the Rio Tolka,
Jim Bowie
whispers in my ear,
and a million long-tailed Mexican bats
dance through a silver-winged
cloud of moths.

We held those borderlands for a week,
exercising our God-given right
to fish pinkeens from the shallows
and swim buck-naked in the deep.

Santa Ana
whispers in my ear,
Remember the Alamo.

Wellmount Avenue Blues

Wore the guitar all summer long,
and on into the winter
walked the avenue in slow-time;
a rock musician looking for a three-chord trick:

all I needed was a large enough mirror. Christmas day
the next-door neighbour's twelve-year-old
presented her new guitar for tuning:
the silence echoed down the avenue.

In Herbert Park

'A medley of seafood, prawns and crab', a carton of
'Café Americano Grande',
presented in a well-designed
paper carrier bag, biodegradable.

In Herbert Park the publicly pampered mallard
perform under a scrim of weeping willow.
Above, a heron grooms her outstretched wing,
breaks time
into manageable pieces
blinks, creates a city backdrop.

'Giv' is yer bleedin' walleh
or I'll burst ye.'
I offer him a haiku
and half a sandwich.
'Are ye fuckin' mad or wah.'

A full December sun turns
golden leaves to still life.
Now the heron pierces
still water, a child
throws crumbs in the air
and shouts 'din-din'.

Seated round the pond in studied nonchalance:
books and breadcrumbs,
all the props in place.

Veronica

Hey diddle diddle, the cat
And the fiddle,
The cow jumped over...

She has lost her rhyme,
She has lost her song.

Acanthus, Adiantum, Agapanthus,
Anthemis, Antirrhinum...

All that's left is rote.

Tomorrow, to be plucked from the Tolka waters.
Today, rain-soaked, urine-stained, sitting
In the Botanic Gardens, Glasinevin,
Reciting her passion.

Acanthus, Adiantum, Agapanthus,

Day-trippers with salt and vinegar on their minds
Walk past a tuneless moon,
Look for a rhyme to fill.

Anthemis, Antirrhinum...

St John's Ward

Someone said if you live long enough
you learn to understand everything—
like the chaos theory:
a butterfly flaps its wings in a Peruvian forest
and the next thing you know
the garden wall that Uncle John built falls down:
or, that Big Bang thing…right!
But at my mother's hospital bed
I was surprised to learn both her first-born
and the shakings of the bag
were a pair of slappers. Fair enough—
this came from a woman across the way
who at the time of making this revelation
was sitting strapped to a chair,
a used incontinence pad on her head
and when not denouncing my sisters'
virtue, sang at the top of her voice,
Rolf Harris's *Two Little Boys*:
and there's another thing, I never knew
those two little boys came from Vicarstown.

A Freeman in Finglas

The street hemmed and hawed,
shook their heads.
They all agreed it was not right
that a father should bath his kids
instead of drinking pints on a Saturday night.

When he passed the Fianna Fáil
church gate collection
the first Sunday after Epiphany
without paying his dues,
they hemmed

and hawed, and he passed the Fine Gael
church gate collection
the second Sunday after Pentecost.
What were they to do
and him not paying his dues.

On the 1st of May he helped himself.
To fifty pence from the collection box
(for he was a worker) of the Workers Party,
Democratic Left, sometimes Sinn Féin (Official),
Sometimes Labour. *Tiochfidh ár La.*

Writing to Nikita Khrushchev, he told of his pain,
of the green sequined underpants
he kept in his bottom drawer
waiting to come out of the closet,
declaiming, *Tiochfaídh mo LA.*

Dear confused and lonely, do not fret.
Sitting in my dacha on the Volga,
Octobers come and go, and October
never turned to May, so if I don't
offer advice, you'll understand.

44

So what's that got to do with bath nights
in Finglas in Nineteen Sixty Hippy?
Who knows, but he was the first I knew
to wear green sequined underpants walking down
'Cappagh Road' on his way to the 'Bottom of the Hill'.

The pub hemmed and hawed,
shook their heads,
they all agreed it was not right,
that a father should stand near-naked
at the bar, drinking pints on a Saturday night.

Someone in Winter

The grass is wasted and spent,
a field falls to winter.

In the foreground
an intimate scene—
two men touching in communion.
He kneels,
eyes averted from the camera.
He stands,
left hand resting on the other's right shoulder.

Someone
out of shot holds the day in his mouth.

They might be lovers—
if you hadn't read the caption
or spotted the holstered gun
below the right shoulder of the one standing—
you then take in the other pairs in the field.

Suddenly My Mother

A pheasant calls the summer home.
Haws hang over the back lanes of Kinsealy
and like a tattered butterfly looking
for somewhere to fold its wings—
your shallow breath practises a death-sleep.

A cotton sheet anchors you.
But marvel this image:
a sixteen-year-old girl
stands outside a factory gate, slips
into old age by mistake.

Benediction

At sixty my mother still admired
his feet, long, slender and delicate:
pulling off his boots, the
smell of silage filled the kitchen.

Peeling first the right sock,
stroking, now the left,
pale and unblemished,
nails clear and straight.

Shaking her head at
this perfection, taking
his hands for comparison.
Weathered, scarred and worn

from years spent wrestling
barbed wire and bullocks.
Touches her back.
Are ye ready for your dinner?

Voices

after Mary Dorcey

How with this rage shall beauty hold a plea
Whose action is no stronger than a flower?
Shakespeare

i

O God
go back to the beginning.

O Mary
protector of God come out of your grotto,
answer me this, what use are you
to children whose lips are formed around fear.

silence
the creeping wallpaper silence
the shout of Mrs Sweeney next-door silence
the horses along the avenue silence
the bread van delivering in the afternoon
silence…

O child what breath is left?
The bogey man has been and gone
and all the while the lie:
O angel boy the wonder is you smile.

ii

The lie corroded my clamped mouth,
impossible utterance swallowed, cramped,

I spat out a more plausible understanding.
Time was enough for me, whatever about you.

Sitting here in the sun couldn't hear my own self—
How could I hear you?

Unspoken accusations couldn't haul me back
Through my fault, through my own fault,
through my most grievous fault. No—

I don't suppose that's right, but something like,
something…something made of shadows.
You would have me stand in the light
You would, you would have me say, sorry!

i am a woman of ninety
and know as little as you
sitting there with your questions
you always were a foolish boy
your father a foolish man
and your grandfather went to war
but it's not the worst sin
in fact it's not a sin at all
just a way of being yourselves
but to answer your first question
yes i dream no i don't see myself
sitting in this wheelchair
i have never been more than sixteen
with long black hair
sometimes i pretended to be older
when i buried your grandmothers
your grandfathers
and when i lost the baby
and the times your father came home stocious
and when he burst the stitches
and the morning noon and night
so what more do you want to know

Exposure

The photographs are gone:
some you took and carefully
cut with a scissors into small pieces,
some you grabbed carelessly
and tossed in the bin.

You worked your way through four generations:
decapitated some
maimed others
discarded the rest,
not one survived whole.

You were thorough working through
every box and drawer.
When finished
all that was left was the immediate family—
framed, laid out on your bureau.

No one imagined you had the strength
or inclination in your final weeks...
yet there we were, all gathered about
your death bed:
not one of us complete.

Song of My Amazing Trousers (and a red shirt)

Walking down Grafton Street
I turned into one of those side streets
where lads in Nike runners mug you
in a shop window
an amazing pair of trousers
how much are those amazing trousers
I asked the shop assistant
you won't believe it she said
but those amazing trousers
are reduced from £100 to £40
this was years ago and I had never paid
more than £20 for a pair of trousers
can I try them on
sure and she gave me a big smile
as if to say all sorts of things
I put them on
stick them old ordinary trousers in a bag

I walked all over Dublin
and by the way people were looking at me
they could see these were amazing trousers
I forgot to tell you my wife and I
were about to go on holidays to Spain
with our friends Eamonn and Eithne
who had nothing to wear
and I felt really sorry for them
although Eithne bought a very expensive pair of sunglasses in the airport
when we were walking in the foothills
of the Sierra Nevada I fell into a big hole that appeared out of nowhere
and my trousers got covered in dirt
I just clicked my heels and my amazing trousers looked
as if they'd never been down a dirty big hole
and you still couldn't find the secret pocket
if you hadn't been shown it

Near the end of the second week when we'd had enough
of the mountains and really all of us wanted to be home
but we couldn't say that because we were on holidays
I spilt a whole bottle of red wine down my trousers
and hadn't got a sack of salt to rub in
but first thing the next afternoon
I rinsed them under the shower and do you know what
they were as good as new and I found 50,000 pesetas in the back pocket

Back home I was thinking of changing my job
and I read in the paper about how MBNA
were the best company to work for in Europe
so I sent of an application form and they called me for an interview
so I thought I better find out what they do
and it turns out they make credit cards
and you wouldn't think a company making credit cards
would be the best company to work for in Europe
so I went along for the interview wearing my amazing trousers
but I wore a knee-length black coat over them to look neat
and the woman interviewer says to me as soon as I get into the room

why are you wearing a black knee-length coat on such a lovely day
I say
I spilt soup on my shirt
she says
ahh...that doesn't matter you'll be more comfortable with your coat off
so I took off my coat and before I had time to say sorry about lying

she says
they're an amazing pair of trousers
where did you get them
were they very expensive
are they comfortable about the crotch
do they come in other amazing colours

I tell her
I got them in one of those places in Dublin where you go to get mugged
and your credit cards stolen
but that probably wouldn't bother you so much
because you could make some more

they were fierce dear
there's loads of room
they only come in one amazing colour

And didn't I get the job

These trousers are really amazing

Epilogue

Five years later
in a Dallas discount store
All items half price or less
a red shirt
I'd been looking for a red shirt for about twenty years
here I thought is the right one and when I looked at the label

This shirt can be worn anywhere except the office

I bought it for $10
which I reckon was a bargain
even though my daughter had gone off to Texas after college
her an only child and spoilt rotten as it was my duty to do
who when she was six years old said she would marry her daddy
crossed her heart and hoped to die
that she would never leave home
and here she was in Dallas getting up to no good
I think children are very ungrateful
but when I wore this red shirt
over my amazing trousers
honest to god I was twice as amazing